AN EXPLORATION IN PHOTOGRAPHS   THE

WE ARE WHAT WE ARE BECAUSE OF WHERE WE LIVE.

This book is dedicated to the people of the Peace,
that they may love this land even more,
and care for it wisely.

AN EXPLORATION IN PHOTOGRAPHS   THE *Peace*

BY DONALD A. PETTIT

Published in Canada by
photoGraphics
Box 823
Dawson Creek, British Columbia
Canada V1G 4H8
ph: 250-782-6068
email: dpettit@pris.ca
www.pris.ca/photographics
First printing, 2001. Second printing, 2002

National Library of Canada Cataloguing in Publication Data

Pettit, Donald A., 1948-
 The Peace

 Includes index.
 ISBN 0-9687363-1-9

 1. Peace River Region (B.C. and Alta.)--Pictorial works. I. Swail,
Barbara. II. Title.
FC3693.4.P47 2001   917.123'1'0022   C2001-910651-3
F1079.P3P47 2001

Cover and book design by Denis & Muntener Advertising Ltd., Prince George, British Columbia.
Watershed illustration by Barbara Swail.
Printed and bound in Canada by Friesens Corporation, Altona, Manitoba.
Printed with vegetable-based inks on paper containing twenty per cent post consumer waste.

Your comments are welcome.
Enlargements of these images are available from Donald A. Pettit / photoGraphics.

A portion of the proceeds from the sale of this book will help fund environmental research,
restoration and protection projects in the Peace River bioregion.

Acknowledgements

For introducing me to photography and trusting my friends and me with a key to the high school darkroom: Mr. Fred Chidley.

For instilling the self confidence to try anything and to value what's really important, and for the love of nature:
my brother, mother and father.

For leading the way: the many Peace region photographers who have preceded me, including Czeslaw (Chester) Wrzesniak,
who died at 79 in a good way – taking pictures in the mountains.

For keeping me in touch with playful creativity: my students.

For help with this manuscript and book design, patience and support throughout, and a beautiful watershed map: Barbara Swail.

For research and editing: Linda Studley, Wim Kok, Mark Hanen, Day Roberts, Carl Gitscheff, Marilyn Boronowski, Meredith Thornton,
Mary Kate Joensen.

For much needed help with poetry: Donna Kane, George Sipos.

For design and image editing: Roman Muntener, Carol Fairhurst, Laine Dahlen.

For an amazing flight to Wood Buffalo National Park, plus accommodation and friendship there: Stuart Barr, Libby Gunn.

For marketing and media assistance: Cees van de Mond.

For First Nations consultation: George Desjarlais of West Moberly First Nations.

For encouragement and help in countless ways: Gunter Sulek, Doris Miedzinski, Donna MacDiarmid.

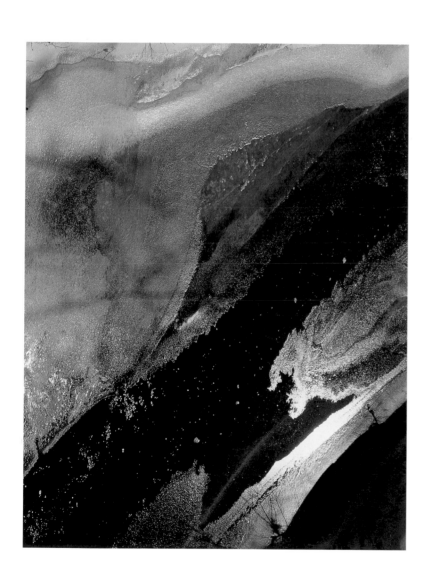

CONTENTS

INTRODUCTION

It is wildness that interests me.

Wildness lives in neglected corners of backyards, in special spots hidden in urban parks, or untrammeled places, free from human mark. The Peace is a generous landscape, bountiful in all of these, but especially the wildest kind of wild.

This is where I most like to be. The camera that takes me there is both reason and method. Looking out through the lens, moving with decisions of composition, viewpoint and exposure, I look inside too, for relationship, insight, and mood. Photographs are bits of these, crystallized.

Looking skyward on a clear night, I can see with my naked eyes two million light years to the great galaxy of Andromeda. The more I know nature, the more I feel part of an intricate, endless web, teaming with life. Like Andromeda, this galaxy of living nature is infinitely wild and distant, yet always there in my own backyard.

A thrilling companionship is waiting to be found in wildness. When I am there, at last, awe-struck by nature's infinite talent, I see the work of the greatest artist of all everywhere I turn. Photographs reach out and capture this, then bring to others the wonderful, simple things I discover.

This book explores the vast and unique Peace River countryside, the wild world I love – the world of Sky, Earth, Water and Life.

PREFACE

THE PEACE BIOREGION

A bioregion is a distinctive area of the Earth defined by the contours and rhythms of nature. Bioregions are usually watersheds, but can also be deserts, mountain ranges, islands or other territories, often reflecting the natural divisions of land used by indigenous peoples, but seldom following the political boundaries we see on maps.

A bioregion has a distinct hydrology, flora, fauna and climate, and for its human inhabitants, a clear sense of place and belonging, a unique culture and unifying economy.

The Peace bioregion is most clearly defined by the watershed of the Peace River, which spans the northern reaches of two Canadian provinces, British Columbia and Alberta. Extending from the Omineca Mountains in the west to Lake Athabaska in the east, from Wood Buffalo National Park in the north to Mt. Robson in the south, the Peace River watershed drains 30 million hectares, an area almost the size of California.

Spawned by melting glaciers high in the Rocky Mountains, then formed by the convergence of the Finlay and Parsnip Rivers, the waters of the Peace first linger in Williston Lake, the reservoir of the WAC Bennett dam. Running swiftly to eastern lowlands, the Peace descends through foothills, then winds its way across the prairies of northeast British Columbia and northern Alberta. Over 1,900 kilometres from its western source, the mighty Peace River joins the Slave River at Lake Athabaska, forming the Peace-Athabasca Delta, one of the largest inland freshwater deltas in the world. From trickling glaciers' melt to broad lowland, the waters of the Peace have descended 3,600 metres by long journey's end.

Merged with the Slave River, the Peace waters travel north to Great Slave Lake and the Mackenzie River, flowing at last into the Arctic Ocean.

COLUMBIA

ALBERTA

Ft. Nelson

INTERIOR PLAINS

Pink Mountain

Beatton

Blueberry R.

Halfway R.

Doig R.

Clear Hills

Notikewan R.

To Yellowknife

High Level

River

Bede Crk.

Paddle Prairie

Boyer R.

Keg R.

Twin Lakes

Meikle R.

Manning

Mackenzie Hwy.

Whitemud R.

Caribou Mtns.

Ponton R.

Fort Vermillion

Bear R.

PEACE RIVER

Wakeman R.

Wolverine R.

Buffalo Head Hills

Little Cadotte R.

Wood Buffalo

Berry Crk.

Jackfish R.

National Park

Harper Crk.

Mikkwa R.

Wabasca R.

Peace Point

River

Birch R.

Alice Crk.

Slave R.

Lake Athabasca

Fort Chipewyan

Lake Claire

Athabasca R.

Birch Mtns.

clear R.

Eureka R.

Cleardale

Ft. St. John

Clayhurst

PEACE RIVER

Fairview

Dunvegan

Peace Reach

Hudson's Hope

RIVER

WAC Bennett Dam

Rolla

Dawson Creek

Moberly R.

Chetwynd

Pine R.

Sukunka R.

Murray R.

Pine Pass

Tumbler Ridge

Kiskatinaw R.

Hwy 2

Beaverlodge

Wembly

Hook Lk.

Monkman Provincial Park

Wapiti R.

MOUNTAINS

Narraway R.

Kakwa Provincial Recreation Area

Kakwa R.

Smoky R.

Cadotte R.

Lubicon R.

Lubicon Lk.

Smoky R.

Spirit River

Bercroft

Bluce Coupe R.

Saddle R.

Sexsmith

Grande Prairie

Falher

Hwy 43

Valleyview

Fox Creek

Little Smoky R.

Simonette R.

Wilbank R.

Grande Cache

Willmore Wilderness Provincial Park

Smoky R.

Muskeg R.

PRINCE GEORGE

To Jasper

Mount Robson Provincial Park

Mount Robson

Jasper

Jasper National Park

Athabasca R.

To Edmonton

S. Heart R.

Whitemud Lk.

Lesser Slave Lake

LANDSCAPE

The Peace River watershed encompasses an amazing variety of physiographic regions, from prairie farmland to wild alpine tundra.

The Rocky Mountains stand as the majestic south and west bastions of the area, creating a barrier to Pacific coastal weather and a unique, drier Peace bioregion beyond. These are young and rugged mountains, only now experiencing the forces that have smoothed and softened the world's older ranges.

Mt. Robson, the highest peak in the Canadian Rockies at 3955 metres, defines the southern tip of the bioregion. Its northern slopes provide the first waters of the Smoky River, a major tributary of the Peace.

The foothills offer a gentler perspective than their big brothers, with verdant forests rolling down to fertile prairies sparsely populated with cities, towns and rural villages.

Now broad and warmed by the microclimate of her own steep banks, the Peace gathers the waters from these low hills and broad prairies, finally moving to the slow rhythm of the Peace-Athabasca Delta boreal plains. These flat lowlands are built on sedimentary bedrock and covered with glacial till, etched in a mosaic of muskeg, meandering streams, shallow lakes, bogs and boreal forests. Here, the waters of the Peace begin percolating through glacial soils and porous bedrock, creating salt plains, sinkholes, and underground streams, as well as some of the most biologically productive freshwater wetlands in the world.

FAUNA

The watershed is home to fifty nine species of mammals, two hundred and fifteen species of birds including over one hundred different song birds, six species of amphibians, two species of reptiles, and twenty nine species of fish.

Here is the densest black bear population in the world, sharing ground with another great bear – the grizzly. Many fur bearers, like beaver, wolf, wolverine, fisher, marten, mink, otter, lynx, muskrat, coyote, fox, squirrel, and weasel (also called ermine when it has its white winter coat) were very important to the early fur trade, and are still plentiful. The beaver, after a long decline, has returned to numbers greater than those recorded by the first European explorers.

Here also live the moose, largest hoofed mammal in Canada. The Peace supports large populations of elk, caribou, mountain sheep and mountain goat, with mule or whitetail deer a part of every rural backyard and roadside landscape.

Bison, once plentiful in the Peace region, have dwindled to a comparatively small population protected in Wood Buffalo National Park, and a successfully reintroduced wood bison population north of the BC Peace. Pure wood bison are found only in Canada, and are federally listed as an endangered species. Bison are, however, making a comeback as livestock animals naturally adapted to this area's climate and landscape.

The Peace River ends at the Peace-Athabaska Delta in Wood Buffalo National Park, a wetland of continental importance. Mallards, American widgeon, American green-winged teal, lesser scaup, ring-necked ducks, and bufflehead as well as grebes, coots, swans and geese dominate the waterfowl community, partly here to breed but mostly for molting and staging. The endangered whooping crane, whose last natural nesting area is in the northern portion of Wood Buffalo National Park, use the Delta during migration, along with hundreds of thousands of waterfowl from all four North American flyways.

Bald eagles and the larger golden eagles are both commonly seen in the mountainous headwaters of the Peace region. Known for its majestic flight, the golden eagle glides and soars with only the occasion beat of its two metre wingspread.

Lake trout, Dolly Varden, rainbow trout, Arctic grayling, Walleye and northern pike are among the important game fish found here in abundance.

FLORA

The Peace River watershed is a complex mixture of unique and diverse ecosystems, each with its own characteristic flora: cactus grow on the dry, south-facing banks of the Peace River valley; delicate orchids fill damp bogs with elusive, exotic fragrance.

A walk in the boreal forest is an adventure in

miniature. Tiny twinflowers produce a delicious fragrance that belies their stature. Shy violets, purple, white or yellow, can be found hiding in the shade. Perky bunchberry flowers, also called dwarf dogwood, carpet large areas with their creamy flowers and bright red berries. Wild strawberry plants offer miniature, incredibly flavourful berries – a treat that dreams are made of.

White and black spruce and lodgepole pine are the predominant conifers. There are scattered pockets of tamarack, also known as larch, the only cone-bearing tree to lose its needles in the autumn. Slender, graceful trembling aspen, balsam poplar, and white birch comprise the majority of deciduous trees.

Rich fragrances adorn each season. Most memorable are the delicate scent of wild rose in spring and early summer, and the tart smell of highbush cranberry each fall.

The summer season may be short if counted in days, but the long hours of daylight extend the growing season dramatically. Peace River wheat is commonly accepted as the best in the world, and the area is famous for its honey. It seems as if plants, knowing the growing season is short, work harder to pack more flavour and sweetness into their fruits, nectar and seeds.

THE SEASONS

"The only people who predict the weather in the Peace River Country are fools and newcomers."

So goes the sage observation of Peace River pioneers, well-acquainted with temperatures of minus 50 degrees Celsius in the winter and 35 degrees in the summer. Chinooks, strong southwest winds that bring a welcome and unexpected taste of spring several times each winter, can raise the temperature from well below freezing to well above in just a few hours.

Spanning the range of 53 to 59 degrees north latitude, the Peace experiences daylight extremes characteristic of the north – the sun barely sets through June and July, and provides only short but sunny days through December and January.

The winter sun is low and shadows long. Night skies are crisp, dark and clear, ideal for stargazing, accented with stunning, colourful displays of northern lights. When temperatures dip to their lowest several times each winter, air moisture condenses and freezes, and ice fogs

coat vegetation and tree tops with crystalline white hoar-frost.

Canada Geese fly in with the spring rains each April, while on the ground below, the month of May is filled with the sound of rushing water and the pungent and heady scent of Balm of Gilead, the resin of the aspen bud. Suddenly the forests are filled with countless song birds, returning to nest after their long and perilous migrations from South America, Mexico and the southern United States. Gardens are traditionally planted on May 24th after the threat of frost is, usually, safely past.

With an average of only 46 cm of precipitation each year, the Peace has modest winter snowfall and relatively dry summers. Long summer days under a hot sun, high in the sky, are punctuated with sometimes fierce thunderstorms. Adequate rain and very long summer hours of sunlight provide an excellent climate for grains, oil seeds, grasses and livestock.

September and October are months of harvest and preparation for winter. Sunny warm days follow frosty, clear nights, while the scent of freshly cut hay and wild cranberries mingle in the air. Autumn in the Peace region is also the sound of crunching leaves underfoot, the honking of thousands of Canada Geese, and the distant drone of farm machinery busy on the land.

EARLY HISTORY

Over one hundred million years ago, a great sea covered the prairies from the Arctic Ocean to the Gulf of Mexico. The Peace River, just a stream then, carried sediments into a dense sub-tropical marsh where the Rocky Mountains are today, helping dinosaurs to live and burying them when they died. Today, the area around Hudson's Hope is rich in their fossil remains.

The Peace River valley was covered by massive sheets of ice during several periods of glaciation. Between sixty and twenty three thousand years ago the area's unique landscape began to emerge as the river that was to become the Peace gouged through the Rocky Mountains, a feat that few rivers have accomplished. Final glacial onslaughts, the Laurentide from the northeast and the Cordilleran from the west, met near what is now Fort St. John.

The 1,100 kilometre long ice-free corridor that formed parallel to the eastern slopes of the Rocky Mountains is thought to be the route by which First Nations people first entered the Americas from the north, an idea supported by scattered archaeological evidence of human occupation in the Peace 10,000 years ago.

As the glaciers melted, rivers and valleys were born. Ice dams created Glacial Lake Peace and Lake McConnell, enormous bodies of fresh water that covered most of what is now the Peace region, depositing a thick mantle of fine silt and clay, the source of the area's present agricultural fertility.

Ten thousand five hundred years ago, the Peace river resumed its unrestricted course as Glacial Lake Peace and Lake McConnell drained, and vegetation changed from arctic tundra to prairie grasslands, with forests of aspen, pine and spruce. Theoretically, Charlie Lake near Fort St. John and Lake Athabasca in northern Alberta are remnants of these glacial lakes.

MAN

As glaciers retreated and the waters once again ran free, the Peace was first inhabited by a variety of indigenous peoples, starting with the Beaver, the Sekani and the Slavey, followed by the Chipewyan, the Cree, and just 100 years ago, the Saulteau. These First Nations people lived a nomadic, hunting and gathering lifestyle, moving from place to place according to their needs and the rhythms of the seasons, living difficult lives but living lightly on the land.

The history of European settlement of the Peace parallels the history of transportation. Among the first Europeans in the area were fur traders for whom the Peace River and its tributaries were vital trade routes. When the Hudson's Bay Company became established in eastern Canada in 1670, repercussions travelled west to the Peace River area in the form of guns and trade goods. The Cree, because they lived closer to the Hudson's Bay Company, obtained guns first, and so pushed the Beaver to the west across the Peace River. In 1781 many of the Beaver Nation died of small pox, a white man's disease, weakening their power once again.

In 1782, a great peace rally was held between the Beaver and Cree on the Peace River at the place known as Unchagah, or Peace Point. With the smoking of the peace pipe, a truce was made, setting the river as the boundary between their hunting territories – the Beaver to the west and the Cree to the east. Today, the Peace watershed is shared by a half dozen or more First Nations.

By the late 1700's the two rival fur trading companies, the Hudson's Bay Company and the North West Company, had reached the Peace River watershed on the heels of explorer Alexander MacKenzie. MacKenzie was a hard-nosed and outspoken Scot who commanded the North West Company post on Lake Athabasca in 1787. Unlike many fur traders, he saw the indigenous people as his greatest asset, and they returned this respect with aid, provisions and advice about this new, wild country.

In 1789, MacKenzie left Old Fort Point, now Fort Chipewyan, in search of the North West Passage. His first expedition led him only to "the river of disappointment," now the Mackenzie River, and to the "Frozen Ocean," the Arctic.

MacKenzie's second voyage to the Pacific in 1792-93 met with success. By canoe from Fort Chipewyan he travelled the Peace River, then the Parsnip, the McGregor and the Fraser Rivers. Finally hiking overland, he arrived on the shores of the Pacific Ocean at Bella Coola, becoming the first white man to traverse the northern continent.

After many years of feuding, the North West Company and the Hudson's Bay Company merged in 1821. A string of trading posts along the Peace became important centres for the northern fur trade. Missions were established here by both Anglican and Catholic churches.

During the 1860's there were some attempts at gold panning on the Omineca and on the Peace with no important finds. Some Klondikers passed through the area on their way to the Yukon Gold Rush in 1898, but it was not a good route to the goldfields.

The 1870's saw surveyors and geologists exploring the Peace in preparation for the Canadian government's plan to build a railway from Ontario to the Pacific. Botanist J. Macoun, surveyor A.R.C. Selwyn and geologist G.M. Dawson all documented the area, taking back reports of fertile soil and favourable climate.

Agricultural settlement began in the 1880's on the Alberta side of the Peace, at Shaftesbury Settlement near the present town of Peace River. In British Columbia, the Peace region opened up after 1912, with settlers from Europe and North America. A hardy bunch, they paid ten dollars each and endured hardships to prove up a claim to a quarter section of Peace River land.

The turn of the century brought the steam-driven paddlewheeler to the Peace River, and an era of luxury transportation to those who could afford it. The largest and most famous of all the Peace sternwheelers was the D. A. Thomas, launched from the West Peace Shipyards in 1916. It featured electricity, hot and cold running water and the finest silverware. With accommodation for 160, it was 49.4 metres long and 11.3 metres wide, and navigated the river for 15 years between Peace River and Hudson's Hope.

Although economic hardship dogged the Peace during the Great Depression of the 1930's, as it did throughout Canada, the area was never plagued by the severe droughts that devastated the southern prairies.

As settlers moved west, the railways were not far behind. For almost 65 years the Northern Alberta Railways Company and its predecessors brought a wealth of forest products, minerals, grain and livestock from the Peace, while sending equipment, fuel and vital supplies back to the north.

Three main pioneer rail lines were involved in the opening up of northern Alberta and northeast BC: the *Edmonton, Dunvegan & BC Railways*, running from Edmonton northwest to McLennan in 1915, and Spirit River and Grande Prairie in 1916; the *Alberta & Great Waterways Railway*, from just north of Edmonton to Lac La Biche in 1915, Waterways in 1922 and Fort McMurray in 1925; and the *Central Canada Railway* to Peace River Crossing (now the town of Peace River) in 1916, Fairview in 1928 and Hines Creek in 1930. The three lines were purchased jointly by the Canadian Pacific and Canadian National Railways and were incorporated under federal charter as the Northern Alberta Railways in 1929. The NAR extended its rails from Hythe, Alberta to Pouce Coupe and Dawson Creek, BC in 1930.

The NAR rail line to Dawson Creek became pivotal in 1942 when Canada and the United States agreed to build a land route to Alaska in response to a perceived threat of invasion from Japan. The Alcan Highway, now known as the Alaska Highway, was built in just 9 months through 2400 kilometres of uncharted muskeg, forest, and mountain – an incredible feat of engineering.

Today the Alaska Highway is a major tourist attraction, with Dawson Creek claiming fame as "Mile Zero." About 350,000 travellers head north on the highway each year, lured by the wild and majestic scenery of northeast BC, Yukon and Alaska.

Immense reserves of oil, natural gas and coal have been discovered under the Peace region, a reminder of our fossil past. The extraction and transportation of these fuels continue to drive much of the area's economy, although in a sporadic fashion that contrasts with the slow growth of the area's more traditional agricultural foundation.

In the mid-1960's the WAC Bennett Dam was constructed near Hudson's Hope, creating Williston Lake and transforming the headwaters of the Peace River. Williston is British Columbia's largest lake, with over 1600 kilometres of wild and mountainous shoreline. Twenty three kilometres downstream, Peace Canyon Dam was later constructed, bringing the total generating capacity of both dams to 3,430 megawatts.

For the first time since the last ice age, the flow of the Peace River is controlled and regulated, affecting the seasonal flooding of globally important wetlands downstream. The environmental impacts of hydro-electric dams, oil, gas and coal extraction, a rapidly expanding forest industry and agriculture are not well documented in the Peace bioregion, but are no doubt significant.

The territory of the Peace watershed is very large and the human population small, but the character of this land is changing rapidly. Thankfully, important provincial and federal parks exist to preserve some of the area's wilderness character. These include the Kwadacha Wilderness Park and Tatlatui Provincial Park at the northern headwaters of the Peace River; Monkman Provincial Park near Tumbler Ridge; Kakwa Provincial Recreation Area and Willmore Wilderness Park in the southern mountains of the watershed; and Wood Buffalo National Park, protecting important boreal lowland habitat and the wetlands of the Peace-Athabasca Delta.

The Peace River watershed defines a unique bioregion with distinct landscape, fauna, flora, climate and history. It remains sparsely populated and rich in wildness – an environment for those drawn to independence, room to move, and the outdoors.

Vast, unique and complex, but to the people who live here, it is simply "the Peace."

Here the sky inhabits us -
moving wind above a dusty floor,
ceiling of clouds,
an architecture of air so open
it breathes the shape of who we are.

Beyond cities
nights fill with stars,
the earth spins
to morning.

In the Peace, sky is more
than half the world.

earth

Glacier etched
a mile under ice
just yesterday,

the hillsides are filled
with the fragrance
of aspen in bud,
of drying leaves.

We too are
land and leaf mould,
a vastness beyond measure.

water

Wing, hoof and hand drink
equally from the river,
cool water flows
to hot pumping blood.

A thousand miles from the city
springs, rain, snow
gather
one drop at a time,
quietly.

After glacier's retreat
and the wetlands of birds
it flows deep, vast and dark
past terraced banks
sparkling under the moon.

life

We are visitors
to this wilderness
of silence.

Black wings beat the rhythm
of storm clouds,
flowers shine beneath our feet
like stars reflecting
in pools of grass.

Life moves quietly, softly
in water,
over land,
through sky.

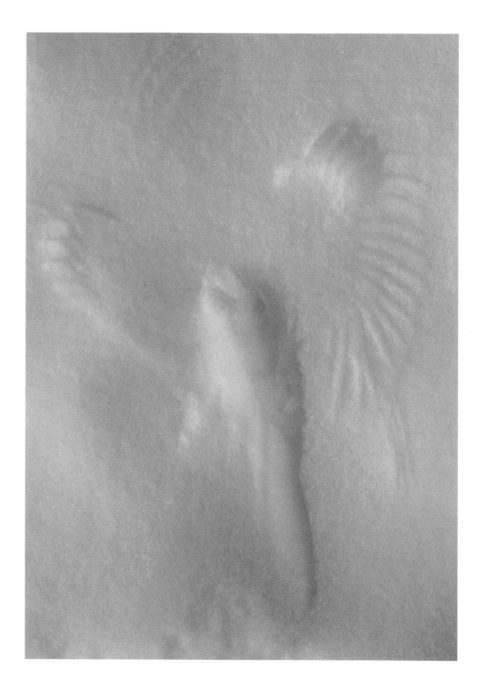

PHOTOGRAPHER'S NOTES

Photography is my passion.

I love that it takes me out into the world and gets me involved. I love the technology of it, the finely crafted cameras and lenses, the way film is kept cool and dark until just the right moment. Precise, focused pulses of light, making images.

I like red-light darkrooms, the glassware and bubbling water, bringing liquid images to life.

I like long timed exposures of the night sky, sitting and watching in the dark, my camera catching and storing occasional photons, slowly building an image from the ancient light of stars.

I like experimenting, perhaps even making little discoveries, and I love strange, accidental images that no amount of skill could ever produce.

I love the magic of photography, and the crisp, reliable reality of it too. I love its usefulness, its ability to precisely record, but also reveal strange, unseen worlds – the infrared and polarized, stopped motion and blurred time, the almost invisible made manifest.

For me, the techniques and technology of photography offer some of its richest rewards. Like the learning of other technical crafts, photography provides the satisfaction of creatively applying acquired tools and knowledge, won after years of study and practice.

My philosophy of photography is simple: manual and mechanical rather than automatic and electronic. Watch out for buttons. If you have more than one or two on your camera, you may have too many. After all, a camera is only a box that lets little bits of light fall on film. The lens simply focuses the light. Almost everything else will just get in your way.

The technology of photography was, I believe, perfected sometime around 1975, if not before. Since then, so-called improvements provide automatic features that promise creative freedom, but deliver instead unnecessary cost, annoying complexity, and reduced reliability. There are, of course, exceptions to this rule, but it is safe to invest time and money in name brand, fully manual, good condition used equipment of the '70 to '80's era, and I recommend this approach to anyone interested in nature photography.

Much of my work is done in 35mm, but many of the full page images in *The Peace* were taken with a Mamiya Pro-S medium format camera that creates beautiful, crisp 6x7 cm negatives or transparencies – five times the size of 35 mm. Everything else being equal, the Mamiya will capture five times the detail and provide enlargements without loss much larger than 35 mm.

The Mamiya Pro-S is a formidable piece of equipment to haul around the countryside (it is usually considered a studio camera) but worth the extra effort. Working with a large instrument that always requires some set-up, lends an air of care and deliberateness to the photographic process that is easily set aside with smaller cameras – a deliberateness that I enjoy and find fruitful.

The Pro-S revolving film back provides vertical and horizontal compositions without moving the camera, and a built-in bellows allows focusing down to an inch or two, perfect for close-ups of wildflowers and other small subjects.

I use only two Mamiya lenses: a wide angle 65 mm lens that features a floating, adjustable element to reduce the distortion of extreme close-ups, and a 127mm medium telephoto that is my favourite for landscapes. These superb lenses feature leaf shutters for vibration-free mirror-up photography. A polarizing filter often helps saturate colour and darken blue skies.

This is an entirely manual, mechanical camera, so there are no batteries to fail in cold weather and no limit to the length of timed exposures. Since the camera has no built-in light meter, a small hand-held Pentax digital spot meter calculates exposures. With it, I accurately meter individual areas of the subject, and using the zone system, place highlights and shadows where I want them. If it feels like an important image, I bracket one stop over and one under the calculated exposure in half-stop intervals. This also provides duplicate transparencies of my best shots . . . as well as some creative surprises.

I shoot from a tripod and use a cable release for maximum clarity, eliminating shutter speed concerns. For years I thought a heavy tripod necessary for such a large camera, but recently a smaller but very sturdy Manfrotto tripod with ball head has proven stable while saving a few pounds – an important feature when heading into the back country.

And of course there is the image size! Working with 6x7 cm transparencies is a true joy, and rapidly becomes addicting. To prevent wear and tear on the original, I will often have a 4x5 inch negative made from the transparency for printing highly detailed enlargements to literally any size.

The smaller images in *The Peace* were shot with a variety of Canon 35 mm single lens reflex cameras, most recently the reliable, simple and inexpensive Canon A1. When moving to this smaller, more versatile format, I happily experiment with a variety of focal lengths: 24 and 28 mm wide angles; 35-70, 70-150 and 100-300 zoom lens as well as a 500mm mirror lens, all Canon and all of the A1 vintage.

Fine grain and colour saturation are the features I look for in transparency films. The wonderful Kodachrome and Ektachrome films have slowly given way, for me, to the livelier Fujichrome slow speed films, settling most recently on Velvia 50. For shooting the northern lights or when using fast shutter speeds with long lenses, Fujichrome 400 provides excellent results. Black and white Kodak Plus-X and Tri-X are still trusted friends, developed and printed in my own wet-chemistry darkroom.

None of the photographs in this book are digitally altered, other than colour balancing and spotting as needed, with the one exception of the digital collage on pages 110-111. This image was pre-visualized and sketched on paper. I then shot hundreds of raven images on conventional black and white 35 mm film and several forest shots on medium format black and white. Selected negatives were scanned, resized and composed in the computer to match my original sketch. Using the computer in this way, an image that lived only in my imagination was brought into reality.

Such manipulation opens exciting creative doors, but the eventual loss of truth and honesty, uniquely associated with the art of photography, must be mourned more than celebrated. Conventional optical/film technologies are proven, stable, very reliable, and of extremely high quality. Replacing them with fully electronic imaging systems will, I fear, shift the photographer's role into the unknown, put him on a perpetual equipment upgrading treadmill, and substitute most photofinishers with automated machines. Today, photography is trusted as a medium that represents truth. In the future, when all images are just so many bits and bytes, this will no longer be the case.

To my students I give this advice: learn the techniques of using a light meter accurately, and perfect the art of exposure; the world is messy, so move in close and fill the frame with your subject, simplifying your image as much as possible; composition is everything, so learn to trust it and work with it; make conscious decisions about depth of focus on every shot; collect pictures you like, study and copy them; to use camera settings creatively they must be understood and therefore set manually – spurn with indignity automatic camera features; photography is all about light, so learn to notice its qualities and how it changes – harshness and softness, reflection and shadow, colour, direction, mood, each season with a light of its own – and be intentional about the light you use.

But most of all, take a lot of pictures. Sounds good, but issues of organization and cost quickly arise. When you are learning and experimenting, boxes of colour prints quickly become awkward and difficult to work with. Slides tell you more about what you are doing, but are more difficult to expose and equally expensive. What to do?

The answer may be a bit surprising: set up a small black and white darkroom in your basement, spare room, or bathroom. Black and white printing and developing in your own darkroom is very inexpensive, easy, fun, and truly a satisfying, hands-on art in itself. Everything you learn in black and white will apply to colour. Most of all, because it is so inexpensive and right there in your own home, it is the key that opens the door to good photography: relentless, prolific picture taking.

Every scene and situation is best evaluated on the spot without reference to record keeping. Indeed, making decisions about exposure, the use of shutter speed to stop or accentuate motion, and f-stop to control depth of focus are far too important for strict rules. For really unusual situations, like shots of the night sky, northern lights, or moonlight scenes where exposure readings cannot be taken, I will, however, make a note of film type, film speed, and camera settings.

The most important notes I keep, however, are written on other pages – a record of the seasons. When do the streams begin to run in the spring; when does the first green grace the spring tree tops; when do the tiger swallowtails first fly in the aspen forest; when is the first frost, the beginning and end of fall colour, the first permanent snowfall? Such a record not only reveals the astonishing regularity of the seasons and life's measured cycles, but proves invaluable when planning outdoor explorations.

More importantly, such a record connects me to where I am. There is a richness that surrounds me, too easily passed by. I have found it best to be where I am and photograph what is around me. I am the world's greatest expert on my own back yard, and surprises lie close at hand.

Photography is a wonderful way to explore the world, and like the other visual arts, it provides practice in truly seeing. Through the eye of the camera, we quickly learn that treasures are everywhere. We need only go out and look.

IMAGE INDEX

53   The folded and twisted rock formations characteristic of the Rocky Mountains, these in Monkman Provincial Park.

54   An old forest fire creates vibrant new growth on the shores of Hook Lake, near Tumbler Ridge.

55   Tiny twinflowers (bottom centre) thrive in the rich mulch of a decaying spruce log.

56-57   A wind-swept crop on the broad prairie farmlands near Fairview.

58   Sun and wind etch crusty ice and snow.

59   Barns like this one near Grande Prairie add grace to the landscape, reminders of an era only recently passed.

60-61   The transition from fall to early winter, where the Kiskatinaw River meets the Peace River near Clayhurst.

62-63   Barley field and barn, icons of the Peace region.

64   The poetry of a smoothly-curved swath line.

65   Barley, an important Peace region crop.

66-67   The warm, orange light and long shadows found just before sunset and just after sunrise create enhanced color and drama.

68   (top) Only the house remains of this homestead near Grande Prairie.
(bottom) The rolling farmland between Dawson Creek and Chetwynd, with flowering canola in the foreground.

69   (top) Canola cut and drying near an abandoned homestead. The city of Grande Prairie is in the far distance.
(bottom) Soft overcast light on this field of barley creates rich color.

70   Aspen forest, after the first frost.

71   A spring meadow near Spirit River, asking to be explored.

Water

72-73   Dark waters of the Peace River reflect silver and gold.

74-75   The steep clay and rock banks of the Kiskatinaw River.

76-77   Kinuseo Falls on the Murray River in Monkman Provincial Park, near Tumbler Ridge. A rare winter view of this 60 metre waterfall.

78-79   Early winter on the Peace River near Clayhurst.

80   Composition with frozen stream and branch.

81   First snow on willow leaves.

82-83   A study in four seasons, where the Murray River meets the Pine River, near Chetwynd.

84   A summer storm sweeps through the Rocky Mountains along the Murray River.

85   Two views of Monkman Lake.

86   Cattails bending.

87   Hook Lake, near Tumbler Ridge.

88   Early summer rain on False Solomon's Seal.

89   Morning mist over Carbon Lake, near Hudson's Hope.

90   (top) Looking toward Finlay Reach, the northern arm of Williston Lake.
(bottom) Peace Reach, the eastern arm of Williston Lake. Here, the Peace River cuts through the Rockies.

91   (top) The Peace River near Clayhurst.
(bottom) The Peace River near Fort Vermilion, broadening as it approaches the Peace-Athabasca Delta.

92-93   Aerial views of the unique Peace-Athabasca Delta in Wood Buffalo National Park. A constantly changing mosaic of muskeg, meandering streams, bogs and boreal forests.

94   A strong north wind has driven wet snow onto one side of every tree. High contrast film enhances the graphic effect.

95   Beautiful Moberly Lake, nestled in the foothills just north of Chetwynd.

96   Crisp, clear and cold, with hoar-frost in the aspen trees.

97   Surrounded by frost, a pine grosbeak pauses.

98-99   The Peace River viewed through a veil of spring leaves, near the town of Peace River.

100   A waterfall on Chesterfield Lake in Kwadacha Wilderness Park at the northern tip of the Peace River watershed. Cow-parsnips (lower right) thrive in this moisture.

101   On the Peace Reach of Williston Lake.

Life

102-103   Yellow warblers.

104-105   Moose, from a hand-coloured black and white print.

106   After the burn, new growth thrives.

107   Heart-leaf arnica.

108   Fireweed, with cow-parsnip in the background.

109   Mule deer.

110-111   This image was assembled digitally from several black and white photographs. A group of ravens is called an "unkindness."

112   Showy aster with first snow.

113   Hoar-frost on aspen tree tops.

114-115 Canada violet, one of the first spring wildflowers.

116   (from top, left to right) Ruffed grouse; American redstart, displaying; evening grosbeak; pine grosbeak, female; young robin's first landing; loon eggs in the nest.

117   (from top, left to right) Stellar's jay; female northern pintail; purple finch; orange-crowned warbler; yellow warblers; American coot dancing across the water. The yellow warblers were photographed from a simple blind constructed just two metres from their nest, from which I seemed to be completely invisible to them. See also pages 102-103.

118   Black-capped chickadee in flight.

119   A suspicious moose casts a wary eye.

120   Fallen cow parsnip covered with snow.

121   (top left) Raven.
(bottom left) Pine grosbeak.
(right) Bird imprint in the snow.

122   Great northern aster. This 4x enlargement reveals the intricate structure of a common wildflower.

123   Tall bluebells (lungwort). These striking blue flowers are just 1.5 cm long.

124   Sometimes you're just in the right place at the right time. I had set up to take a picture of the barn, when a horse suddenly burst forth just as I tripped the shutter. Reproduced from a sepia-toned black and white print.

125   (top) Dawson Creek grain elevators, a memory.
(bottom left) Swathing grain.
(bottom right) Hood ornament in the grass.

126-127 An impressive, skillfully constructed log barn, now abandoned, just north of Dawson Creek.

128   A home-built wheelbarrow.

129   Study in yellow.

130   Late winter sun melts the snow on black pavement.

131   A dry spring.

132   (top) Graineries near Grande Prairie.
(bottom) Livestock shelter, near Fort St. John.

133   Relic found in a field. The chain was skillfully fit to the rock.

134-135 Canadian tiger swallowtail, common to aspen forests in the spring and early summer.

136   Redpoll taking flight.

Photographer's notes

138   Light shines through cattail reeds.

139   (left) Full moon rising at dusk.
(right) The Mamiya medium format camera used to shoot many of these images.

140   (left) Wet birch bark.
(right) Two mule deer almost disappear in the aspen forest.

141   Cattails silhouetted against a frozen pond.

144   Wind-sculpted snow.